Original title:
Island Songs

Copyright © 2025 Creative Arts Management OÜ
All rights reserved.

Author: Helena Marchant
ISBN HARDBACK: 978-1-80581-509-9
ISBN PAPERBACK: 978-1-80581-036-0
ISBN EBOOK: 978-1-80581-509-9

The Serenade of Silvery Waters

A fish named Fred wore a bow tie,
He danced with grace, oh my, oh my!
The crabs all clapped in their own way,
As jellybeans floated, come what may.

The seagulls sang in a high-pitched tone,
While barnacles practiced their best moan.
A dolphin laughed, did a summer flip,
As sandcastles joined in the funny trip.

Corners of Coastal Calm

A turtle tried to take a stroll,
With flip-flops on, he lost control!
The tide pulled back, then sprung ahead,
And off he went, oh dear, oh dread!

The starfish held a fancy feast,
Inviting all from west to east.
A sea cucumber wore a crown,
While waves came crashing, round and round.

A Song of Riptide Reflections

A clam was playing hide and seek,
With a bright pink sock, oh what a peak!
The fish all snickered, a bubbly cheer,
As waves arrived, with splashes near.

The sunset painted the ocean's grin,
As seaweed twirled, a spin within.
A crab named Larry sang a tune,
While clouds drifted like a big balloon.

Wandering Waves

A wave wore sunglasses, cool and sly,
While surfers zoomed, oh me, oh my!
The sand was hot, like popcorn popped,
As beach balls bounced, and laughter hopped.

The octopus juggled seashells bright,
While dolphins twirled in pure delight.
The tide tickled toes on the shore,
And all the sea creatures yelled for more!

Cadences of the Untouched Sands

There once was a crab in the sun,
With dreams of a race, oh what fun!
He'd sprint on the shore,
While gulls laughed in score,
His shell was the prize, just begun.

A fish tried to dance on dry land,
But flopped with a slap of his fin hand.
The crabs started cheer,
"Keep swimming, my dear!
In waters, you'll surely expand!"

The seagulls, they spun in a spree,
With sandwiches stolen, oh me!
They squawked with delight,
As they took an airborne flight,
What a feast for the finned jubilee!

A starfish was stuck in the sand,
He whispered, "I need a new plan,"
With a flip and a twist,
He just couldn't resist,
To wave at the waves, oh so grand.

Songs of the Celestial Horizon

The sun peeked from behind a cloud,
As dolphins danced, lively and loud.
They jumped and they sang,
With a splash and a clang,
Creating a carnival crowd.

A parrot in shades on a tree,
Called out, "Come and join me for tea!"
With fruits piled up high,
And none asking why,
They feasted with laughter and glee.

The stars joined the party at night,
With glowing smiles, oh what a sight!
They twinkled and swayed,
As if serenade,
To the waves that would shimmer so bright.

A turtle played chess with a seal,
Debating on what was the deal.
With moves slow and wise,
They'd plot and surprise,
In a world where the silly was real.

Tidal Whispers

The tide came in like a joke,
And nudged every ship with a poke.
They giggled and swayed,
In a watery parade,
Singing songs that the seagulls bespoke.

A clam tried to catch every wave,
But his efforts turned into a rave.
He flipped on a shell,
With laughter, oh swell,
As the squids would squirt ink to save.

A shrimp took a break with a friend,
They plotted their pranks to upend.
With bubbles that burst,
And outlandish thirst,
For the fun that they never could end.

The breeze carried whispers of cheer,
As fish tales grew grander each year.
With jokes from the deep,
That would make you leap,
In the splashy blue atmosphere.

Melodies of the Sea

A mermaid strummed songs from her rock,
While sea turtles danced 'round the clock.
With seaweed in hand,
They formed a cool band,
And everyone joined in the mock.

A whale trumpeted tunes loud and clear,
With dolphins all swimming near.
They choreographed moves,
With joyous grooves,
Making music that all could endear.

An octopus played with eight arms,
Creating sweet rhythms and charms.
With tentacles bright,
He danced through the night,
In the glow of the ocean's alarms.

The seafoam would whisper and sigh,
To the laughter that flew by the sky.
In the heart of the waves,
Where the silly misbehaves,
The melodies soared, oh so high.

Poetry of the Moonlit Marsh

In the marsh where frogs wear hats,
Crickets tap dance with chatter bats.
A heron juggles fish with flair,
While turtles gossip without a care.

Fireflies twinkle like disco lights,
As owls debate the silliest sights.
The reeds are swaying with great delight,
In this marsh, everything feels just right.

The moon winks down at the mud and muck,
As a raccoon plays peek-a-boo with luck.
Frogs croak out a symphony, it's true,
Making magic under the sky so blue.

In this realm of mirth and glee,
I wonder if they laugh at me!
With each splash and every squeak,
The marsh lives its life, uniquely chic.

Soliloquy of the Seafoam

Upon the shore where foamy waves,
Do a dance that even mermaids crave.
Seagulls squawk with comic flair,
While crabs perform their funny stare.

A starfish tells jokes to passing sand,
While clams give pearls away, unplanned.
The tide rolls in like a giggling child,
Making the sea look ever so wild.

With seaweed wigs all tangled and tossed,
They laugh at the shore, where no one's lost.
A fish forgot how to swim upstream,
And joins the party in frothy dream.

So come on down, let's join the spree,
With waves that swirl and shout with glee.
In this funny world where we frolic and play,
The seafoam sings the best cabaret!

Sweet Serenades of Shimmering Waters

Beneath the waves where bubbles rise,
Fish sing sweet tunes, oh so wise.
With a splash and a swirl, they practice their craft,
While turtles chuckle, their voices a laugh.

The minnows make waves, their tails all a-flick,
While octopuses juggle with a clever trick.
They twirl and spin, all in good jest,
In shimmering waters, they feel truly blessed.

Whales Hum their tunes, a chorus so deep,
As dolphins leap in joyous leaps.
Each note a splash, a giggle, a cheer,
In this watery world, there's nothing to fear.

So dip your toes in the liquid delight,
Join the fishy choir under the light.
With every ripple, they sing from the heart,
In shimmering waters, it's a playful art!

Chronicals of the Roaring Tide

The tide rolls in with a roar and a rumble,
As clowns of the sea start their antics, a jumble.
Seashells gossip on the sandy shore,
While the tide giggles, always wanting more.

Barnacles knit tales of the great blue sea,
While dolphins flip high, just to agree.
With each wave crashing and splashing about,
They laugh at the ocean, daring it out.

A crab plays tag with a nearby fish,
In this wild game, one simply can't wish.
With tides that wave and holler with pride,
The chronicle unfolds with each joyful glide.

So grab your floaties and join the fun,
In laughter and splashes, we're all just one.
The roar of the tide is full of delight,
As we play with the sea from dawn until night!

Sunlit Serenades

In the sun, fish dance so bright,
Crabs in tuxedos, what a sight!
Jellyfish float, waving their hands,
While sea turtles form rock bands.

Seagulls squawk a catchy tune,
Playing chess with the afternoon.
A dolphin jumps, takes a bow,
As beach balls roll from every prow.

Kids on the sand build castles tall,
While the waves giggle, ready to sprawl.
A beach umbrella steals the show,
Dancing around like a disco pro!

Sunset paints the sky in red,
While sandcastles rest their heads.
A clam claps to close the day,
With beachgoers laughing away.

Rhythms of the Reef

Beneath the waves, a party greets,
Where clownfish dance on silly beats.
Starfish clap with all their might,
While sea anemones sway left and right.

Octopuses juggle seashells high,
As seaweed waltzes, oh my, oh my!
A pufferfish blows up with glee,
Singing karaoke under the sea.

Schools of fish swim in a line,
Wiggling their fins like the grand design.
Crustaceans snap to the funky sound,
With boogie moves all around.

At dusk, the reef sparkles bright,
With glowing creatures in the night.
A conch-shell DJ spins the tune,
While the ocean groves under the moon.

The Soundtrack of Silent Shores

On silent shores where whispers play,
The waves are puns, come out to stay.
Seashells laugh, they have a joke,
Even the breeze gives a soft poke.

A sandpiper twirls, it's quite the show,
Digging in sand to find hidden dough.
With crabs that tap dance, clapping their claws,
Nature's orchestra without a pause.

Seagulls take turns on a stage so grand,
With fish in tuxedos, the weirdest band.
A whispering tide hums out a tune,
As starry skies wink like a cartoon.

Sandy toes and flippy flops,
Count the waves, never stops.
A mermaid scoffs, "Try harder now!"
The soundtrack plays; just take a bow!

Driftwood Dreams

Driftwood floats on the azure sea,
Waving hello, come dance with me!
Seagulls giggle, spinning around,
As the shell choir joins in sound.

A lazy fish wears a sunhat wide,
Sipping sea soda, a chilled tide.
Turtles play leapfrog, what a laugh!
While the lone otter takes a bath.

Sandcastles sporting quirky crowns,
Compete with crabs for funniest frowns.
A palm tree shakes its frond in glee,
Baring its coconuts for all to see.

With sunset colors painting a dream,
Dancing waves shimmer and gleam.
Tomorrow's fun, it will not fail,
As driftwood tells its funny tale.

Sheltered Refrains

On a beach that's full of sand,
A crab scuttles, oh so grand.
He waves his claws with a funny flair,
While seagulls squawk like they just don't care.

A coconut fell with a thud,
Hit my head, now I feel the flood.
I dance with fish, a silly sight,
Splashing water, what pure delight!

Turtles giggle as they slide,
Into the waves, oh what a ride!
In the sunshine, we share a grin,
It's a joy where the laughter begins.

As the sunset paints the sky,
I join a frisbee flying high.
Oh, the fun in this merry land,
Where joy and laughter go hand in hand.

Celestial Curations

Starfish lounging on the shore,
As the moonlight starts to pour.
A fishy tale that's quite absurd,
Whispers secrets without a word.

The dolphins dance in the night,
Twinkling stars, what a fancy sight!
But one got tangled in a net,
And flopped about, a funny pet.

Laughter echoes through the tide,
A crab in sunglasses takes a ride.
Through waves that swirl, we cheer and jest,
In this paradise, we're truly blessed.

As the tide pulls in and flows out,
The moon's unique, there's no doubt.
With whimsies stowed in our nets,
We gather memories, no regrets.

Pebble Skimmed Harmonies

With pebbles tossed across the bay,
I try to skip but they just lay.
A frog jumps in; what a surprise!
He ribbits out a comical cry.

A parrot cackles, oh what a show,
Squawking tales of long ago.
Under palm trees, shadows play,
While crabs are dancing, hip-hip-hooray!

I found a shell, it looked so cute,
But it had a snail in pursuit.
We laughed until the sun ran free,
In harmony with the sea's esprit.

As twilight falls, we sing along,
The ocean hums a silly song.
In this whimsical place of glee,
We're the stars of our revelry.

A Dreamer's Dance on Water

A paddleboard wobbles in the breeze,
I'm balancing like I'm on my knees.
The fish below giggle and splash,
As I try to stand, oh what a crash!

With every wave, I sway and spin,
The sea's my stage, let the fun begin!
Seagulls squawk with delightful cheer,
As I sip my drink, oh dear, oh dear!

The sunset's glow brings a vibrant light,
I dance with dolphins, what pure delight!
In a whirl of laughter, we twirl around,
While the ocean serenades the joyous sound.

At the end of this playful spree,
I drift away in sheer glee.
With dreams as wild as waves depart,
I hold this magic close to my heart.

Serene Horizons

On a sand heap, crabs dance around,
With little top hats, they're so profound.
Seagulls squawk jokes, they're quite the jest,
Stealing my chips, they crave a feast.

In the sun, sunburns thrive,
A lobster in shades, oh my, how they jive.
Waves crash in laughter against the shore,
What's this? A sunbather? Just a snack for more!

Flip-flops flapping, a race to the sea,
Who knew my hat would fly away with glee?
A turtle chuckles, slow but spry,
Waving his flipper, "Hey, come and try!"

As the day dips low, the skies turn bright,
We mix silly cocktails, what a sight!
Barrels of laughs, and a fun little song,
In our own world, where we all belong.

Harmonies of the Horizon

Bamboo flutes play the tune of a breeze,
While palm trees sway like they aim to tease.
A parrot croons, with flair and styles,
While I just grin, shedding all my miles.

Sandy toes join in dance, oh so spry,
While starfish whisper, "You should give it a try!"
The sun sings softly, a golden delight,
Mermaids giggle, planning their night.

The ocean waves snap, like the best of friends,
Spilling laughter, as everyone bends.
Shells laugh loudly as they roll on by,
"Oh, the stories we tell in the blink of an eye!"

With ukuleles strumming, we join the fun,
Counting the stars, and dances begun.
As day fades gently into night so warm,
We'll serenade the moon, it's our charm!

The Ballad of the Boundless Blue

A fish in a bow tie swims with flair,
Winking at dolphins, quite the pair.
They plot silly pranks on a passing boat,
"Watch out, there's seaweed on your coat!"

The sun winks down; clouds take a seat,
As we challenge waves to a race, so sweet.
Lost sunglasses float like ships on the seas,
While mermaids munch snacks, swaying with ease.

Riding the swells like a rollercoaster,
Giggling with joy, we become coastbusters.
Every splash a laugh, every bubble a cheer,
In a sea of smiles, troubles are sheer.

Even the jellyfish join in a jig,
As octopuses twist, dancing so big.
Underneath the stars, the night shines bright,
In a rhythm of joy, we delight in the night.

Notes from a Forgotten Cove

Here in the nooks where the wild things hide,
Laughter erupts like the playfully tide.
A crab plays guitar, its claws in a strum,
While a clam hums along, oh what a drum!

Mangroves nod, with secrets to share,
Whispers of seashells, floating in air.
Feathered friends join with a chorus and dance,
Oh, the silly leaps like a spooked little prance!

A snoozing seal makes a pillow of sand,
Every snore triggers a wave so grand.
While I stretch and trip, laughing at fate,
Stumbling through fun, all our worries abate.

As twilight descends, we gather so near,
With goofy faces, we banish all fear.
In this forgotten cove, joy's the prize,
Where humor and quirks light up the skies!

The Rhythm of Sandy Footprints

Barefoot dancers on the shore,
Twisting, twirling, wanting more.
Crabs take a chance, join the beat,
Shaking their claws, oh what a treat!

Waves clap hands in playful cheer,
Seagulls swoop, as if they hear.
A coconut drops, causing a splash,
We giggle, burst, then off we dash!

Sunsets wink with golden eyes,
While flip-flops fly, oh how they fly!
Laughter echoes, silly and bright,
In this dance, we lose the night.

So join the fun, don't hesitate,
Bring your joy, let's celebrate!
With sandy footprints left behind,
Finding rhythm, oh how we bind.

Tunes of the Tropical Twilight

The palm trees sway, a gentle sway,
Thinking they're musicians, come what may.
Chorus of chimes in the warm breeze,
Crickets chirp like they're trying to please.

Laughter blends with the ocean's roar,
As we shake our hips on the sandy floor.
A pineapple hat makes us all grin,
Tropical fashion, where do we begin?

The sun is a DJ spinning tracks,
While we juggle coconuts for laughs and quacks.
Moonlight joins with a wink and a nod,
As we dance like it's the dance of the gods!

So raise your glass filled with bright fizz,
Toast to the tunes, the joy, and the whiz.
Under the stars, we swing and sway,
Tropical twilight, please forever stay!

Songs from the Sheltered Cove

In the cove where laughter's found,
Waves whisper secrets, soft and sound.
Fish goggle-eyed at our silly song,
Wondering if they, too, belong.

Driftwood guitars strum with glee,
As jellyfish float along in spree.
With seashells clapping their tiny hands,
We sing of treasures and far-off lands.

Mirthful echoes bounce from rock to rock,
While sea turtles join in to mock.
A hermit crab dons a tiny crown,
Wiggling and dancing, never a frown.

So gather close for a merry tune,
Under the watchful glow of the moon.
With each chorus, more smiles are brewed,
In our sheltered cove, there's nothing to feud.

Verses of the Crimson Sunset

When the sun starts to blush, oh what a sight,
We grab our snacks, prepare for the night.
Marshmallows roasting with laughter so pure,
A chocolate river, we make, that's for sure!

The sky paints a mural, colors anew,
As we forget what we thought that we knew.
With giggles galore, and stories to share,
Silly tales spun with utmost flair.

As shadows grow long, we dance in the light,
Chasing the laughter that feels just so right.
The stars peek out, twinkling with glee,
We sing with abandon, just you and me.

So let's raise a cheer for the day's grand end,
With crimson hues and all of our friends.
Life's a collection of moments we find,
In verses of sunset, joy intertwined.

The Melody of the Mist

In the fog, the seagulls squawk,
While fishermen dance, they can't just walk.
Their nets are tangled, what a sight,
As boats go wobbling, oh what a fright.

A crab in a tux gives a silly wave,
While waves crash down, they misbehave.
The lighthouse blinks a cheeky grin,
Guiding lost sailors, oh where to begin?

With each splash, a joke is told,
The fishes laugh, both young and old.
The mist may hide, but joy will rise,
With every note, the laughter flies.

So join the fun in this misty haze,
With quips and tunes that warm the days.
Together we sing, with spirits blessed,
In a world where humor is the best.

Harmony in Hidden Harbors

In a cove where shadows play,
A crab conducts in a silly way.
With fishy friends, they start a band,
Strumming seaweed, isn't it grand?

A walrus sings with a voice so low,
While dolphins spin in a watery show.
The boats bob along, they catch the beat,
Making a ruckus with their shuffling feet.

Seagulls squawk like they're in a tune,
Floating around, they twirl with the moon.
Every wave holds a chuckle or two,
As they harmonize under skies so blue.

So come find joy in these secret bays,
Where giggles tumble through sunny rays.
In this harbor, laughter is the key,
Unlocking fun for you and me.

Crescendo of the Coastline

On cliffs where the wild wind plays,
There's a concert of laughter that never decays.
The waves roll in, like a feathered dance,
As crabs on a mission twirl in a prance.

Jellyfish sway in a jelly-like trance,
While starfish cheer, they take a chance.
The gulls are the crowd, they clap their wings,
As the sea sings a tune that joyfully clings.

Each splash and crash runs riotous cheer,
Like a wacky parade, drawing you near.
The sun sets low, spilling golden glows,
While the shoreline hums, where laughter flows.

Join in the fun as night starts to fall,
The coastline's crescendo invites us all.
In this sound, may we find our bliss,
A melody wrapped in a funny twist.

Coastline Cadences

In the morning light, the gulls are bold,
They argue over breakfast, oh what a holed!
With pastries flying, the crabs run fast,
In this quirky dance, there's joy unsurpassed.

Surfboards wobble as surfers shout,
Their balance tips, as they twist about.
A splash and a giggle, off they go,
Riding the waves, like a show in a zoo.

Seashells line the shore, all in a row,
Singing sweet songs, as the tide starts to flow.
Each footstep marks a rhythm on sand,
Creating a beat, so lively and grand.

So come share the laughter, let's sway to the tune,
As the sun dips low and the stars commune.
In these coastal cadences, let's dance and sing,
For in every wave, there's joy to bring.

The Anthem of Sandy Shores

Beneath the sun, we dance around,
With flip-flops flapping on the ground.
Seagulls squawk, they steal our fries,
We laugh until we've teary eyes.

Beach ball bounces, oh what a sight,
Someone's nose is turned so bright!
Sunscreen splatters, laughter so loud,
We're the silliest, sun-kissed crowd.

Surfboards wobble, splashes fly,
Tiny crabs in suits, oh my!
Chasing shadows, drawing lines,
Every footstep, joy defines.

As dusk approaches, fires ignite,
S'mores and giggles, pure delight.
We sing our tune, a joyful fuss,
On sandy shores, it's all of us.

Lyrical Lagoon Lullabies

In a lagoon where fish are friends,
We spin our tales, where laughter blends.
A pelican wears our missing hat,
It's not a bird, it's just a brat!

Splashing water, who made that splash?
Was it a dolphin or a fishy crash?
As seaweed tickles our toes so bright,
We dance with crabs beneath moonlight.

Tangled nets and boats askew,
We laugh until the night turns blue.
Oh, the funny sights we see,
In our lagoon, it's all carefree.

With bubbles floating to the stars,
Even mermaids laugh at our cars.
So here's to songs of silly cheer,
In our lagoon, we shed a tear.

Footprints in the Sand

Each footprint tells a tale of fun,
Lost in laughter, we forget to run.
Kites tangled up in salty breeze,
Even sandcastles break with ease.

Crabs parade in a marching band,
We mimic them, it's quite the stand!
Sunhats flying, sunscreen glops,
Watching our ice cream melt and plop.

A dog runs past with joyful glee,
And steals my sandwich, oh dear me!
Rolling waves, they'll serenade,
As we giggle at the blunders made.

As the tide washes away our trace,
We leave behind a jolly space.
Footprints washed, but joy remains,
In our hearts, the laughter gains.

The Poetry of the Piers

On rickety piers, we sway and sway,
Fish jump, then flop, in disarray.
A seagull steals our picnic spread,
While we chase shadows, laughing instead.

Lines and hooks all tangled tight,
What's this knot? A fishy fight!
With each cast, we hope for gold,
But catch old sneakers—unfold the bold!

Sunshine sparkles on laughter's face,
While old folks nap in a cracking case.
Strumming ukuleles, off-key tunes,
The music dances with the afternoon.

As the sun dips low, we share a grin,
While catching fireflies as night wears thin.
The piers whisper of dreams and plays,
In this funny world, our hearts will stay.

Salty Air and Song

The seagulls squawk, they steal my fries,
A salty breeze, oh what a prize!
With sunburned noses, we dance and sway,
As crabs join in the beachside play.

The sandcastles crumble, but we don't care,
We'll laugh like kids, without a dare.
Fiddles play tunes on a driftwood stage,
The ocean's waves turn every page.

Twirling with shells, we skip along,
In flip-flops, we shuffle to the song.
With every splash, we try to sing,
Ocean melodies, oh what they bring!

So grab your mates, let's lift our drinks,
In this salty air, who really thinks?
With every laugh and every cheer,
We'll serenade, let joy appear.

An Aria Beneath the Banyan

Underneath the banyan tree's sway,
A monkey steals my hat today.
In this leafy stage, we must perform,
As breezes tussle, nature's norm.

The wild duet of chirps and squawks,
A toe-tapping beat as nature walks.
I sing off-key, but who's to know?
The ants in line put on a show!

With lemonade sips and silly grins,
We laugh at life and all its spins.
A picnic spread with snacks galore,
Even the insects join the score!

So gather 'round, we'll make a scene,
Beneath the branches, it's quite serene.
With every laugh, I sing a note,
In this leafy place, joy is remote.

Twilight Tunes

As the sun dips low, we hum a tune,
The fireflies dance, it's a joyous boon.
With every flicker, we tap our feet,
Under the stars, the night feels sweet.

The sand is warm, the waves retreat,
We're barefooted bandits, that can't be beat.
With giggles echoing in the dark,
Even the crickets join our lark.

A ukulele strums with a cheerful sound,
As laughter bounces all around.
We'll croon about the day that's gone,
And dream of the adventures at dawn.

So here's to twilight in every shade,
To funny moments that never fade.
With every strum and every cheer,
We'll sing our joy, loud and clear.

The High Tide Ballad

The waves come crashing with a mighty roar,
I lost my flip-flop right by the shore!
A surfboard's dancing, it's quite a sight,
As seagulls plot to steal my bite.

We build a raft with driftwood pride,
Trying to float, in a kiddie ride.
With laughter spilled upon salty mist,
Every splashed face, simply can't resist.

A conch shell trumpet, my best friend calls,
As we make waves with cannonballs.
In tangled hair and sunburned cheeks,
We find our rhythm, in playful streaks.

So come along, let's make a splash,
With every hiccup, our memories stash.
In frothy fun, we'll serenade,
This high tide ballad, our hearts displayed.

Serenade of the Palm Fronds

Under the fronds, a parrot squawks,
He dances around in flip-flop socks.
A crab joins in with a funky groove,
As coconut water starts to move.

The palm trees sway, they wave goodnight,
As lizards play tag under soft moonlight.
A breeze whispers secrets, oh so sly,
While jellyfish waltz, floating by.

With every sway and every twist,
The hammock swings, we can't resist.
The stars above begin to blink,
Would that be a sign? Let's have a drink!

So gather round the glowing fire,
With tales of mermaids and pirate choir.
Let laughter roll up to the skies,
In this funny dance, no one's shy.

Melodies from the Forgotten Lagoon

In depths where seaweed sways like hair,
Fish sing ballads without a care.
A dolphin's laugh rings clear and loud,
While clams cheer on, they're quite the crowd.

The sun sets low, making shadows long,
A turtle hums an ancient song.
Octopus taps his tentacle beat,
With jellyfish twirling, running on feet.

The hermit crabs march in a line,
Carrying shells that brightly shine.
They stumble and fall, then start to tease,
Get back, you guys, it's just a breeze!

In the magic of the evening light,
Every splash becomes a delight.
With a splashy laugh and a wink of the eye,
The lagoon's a party, oh my, oh my!

Lullabies Beneath the Coconut Canopy

Underneath the trees, so wide and grand,
Squirrels debate who will win the stand.
A coconut rolls, they all take chase,
As geckos giggle with grinning face.

The breeze hums soft, a gentle song,
While crickets chirp all night long.
Fireflies twinkle, they play hide and seek,
While lightbulb bugs glow, not a word they speak.

The moon peeks down, with a sleepy grin,
Watching squirrels as they tumble and spin.
A sloth joins in, with a slow-motion sway,
He thinks he's fast, but it's just not his way!

So come, lie down on the sandy floor,
And listen closely to nature's roar.
With dreams of chuckles to guide our night,
Sleep tight my friend, till morning light.

Chants of the Gentle Currents

The waves chant low, a bubbly hum,
While sea turtles join the whimsical drum.
A fish slips by with a glance and grin,
Winking at waves as they frolic in.

The current flows, a tickling race,
With snorkelers laughing, caught in the chase.
Starfish applaud with a slow, bright flair,
As crabs high-five, without a care.

The seagulls swoop, yelling loud, oh dear!
Mixing up phrases that we can hear.
"Hey! Don't take my sandwich!" one does squawk,
While pelicans holler and take a walk.

In this salty ballet, playfully spun,
Nature's big joke — we're all just for fun.
With giggles and splashes, the ocean sings,
In the heart of the sea, joy brightly springs.

The Rhapsody of Retreat

A crab danced a jig on the shore,
It tickled the toes of a passing boar.
With a splash and a flick, oh what a sight,
They both shared the joy as the day turned to night.

Seagulls squawked in a curious tune,
While a fish wore a hat made of bright balloon.
The sun winked down between giggles and screams,
As the tide played its tunes, like silly old dreams.

A palm tree swayed, showing off its flair,
It tickled the waves with a breezy hair.
The sand called for feet to come have some fun,
With laughter and giggles, we danced in the sun.

So here in this dance, let the laughter ring,
As we twirl with the fish, and we laugh and we sing.
For the joy of retreat is a sweet, silly song,
Where we jive with the crabs and feel we belong.

Canzones of the Crane

A crane in the dusk wore a tutu bright,
It flapped and it twirled, quite a ridiculous sight.
With a squawk and a stomp, it led quite the show,
As frogs joined in chorus, to dance in a row.

The reeds played along with a rustling hum,
And turtles all bobbed, saying, "Where's our drum?"
Each note made a splash, pure hilarity's claim,
As the pond turned to stage, and it joined in the fame.

The water was rippling with laughter and glee,
As a fish pulled a prank on a wise old bumblebee.
With a thud and a splash, oh the chaos flew high,
As the crane took a bow, reaching up to the sky.

So join in the dance of this silly brigade,
Where the music of nature won't ever fade.
Open your hearts, let the giggles take flight,
With the crane and the frogs 'neath the soft moonlight.

Sounds of the Shimmering Sands

A sandcastle tall wore a crown made of shells,
That whispered and giggled with stories it tells.
It swayed to the rhythm of waves rolling by,
While crickets kept time with a chirp and a sigh.

The breeze tossed a feather that fell near a clam,
Who opened its mouth to say, "I'm the man!"
With a wink and a wiggle, it joined in the fun,
As laughter erupted like rays from the sun.

The grains danced in sync with a jig on the beach,
While a dog chased a wave, no joy out of reach.
With sand in their paws and a splatter of foam,
The beach became home; yes, we danced and we roamed.

So hear the sweet sounds where the good times expand,
Each giggle and splash from the shimmering sands.
Let the rhythm consume you, join in the spree,
For the heart of the shore sings as wild and as free.

A Cavern of Sound

Inside of a cave where the echoes played tricks,
A bat wore a monocle, pondering flicks.
As rocks began rolling with laughter and cheer,
They formed into notes, oh so pleasing to ear.

A shadowy figure with whiskers so grand,
Purred melodies softly, a wild serenade.
The waves crashed outside while the lizards would dance,
In a chorus of chuckles, they took every chance.

The stalactites jingled with every soft tune,
While the crickets all stomped, dancing 'round like a moon.
Each ripple of laughter rang out through the night,
And the cave felt alive with a giddy delight.

So gather your friends 'neath this cavernic dome,
Where the songs are a riot, we're never alone.
With laughter and echoes, we'll sing right along,
In this joyful place, where all notes are a song.

Memories Carried by the Tide

Seagulls squawk in a silly dance,
As crabs try out their sideways prance.
The ocean waves laugh with glee,
Telling tales of a wobbly bee.

Flip-flops chase a beach ball's flight,
While sandcastles wobble in delight.
Sunburned noses, red and round,
As the tide pulls the laughter down.

Fish in tuxedos swim with flair,
While dolphins giggle in the salty air.
Shells hold secrets of sandy schemes,
Drifting away like misplaced dreams.

With every splash, a joke is thrown,
In surfboards' antics, joy is grown.
An octopus waves its many arms,
As the shore sings out its colorful charms.

Nocturnal Harmonies of the Deep

The moonlight winks with a mischievous grin,
As fish have parties where seaweed spins.
Crabs in tuxedos check their clocks,
Just in time for the sea turtle's talks.

Underneath, the oysters sing,
In harmonies that the jellyfish bring.
A porpoise jokes, flicks water with flair,
While clams share secrets without a care.

The stars twinkle like big-eyed shrimps,
Telling tales of nightly blimps.
Light from the lighthouse begins to sway,
As conch shells echo, "Hey, let's play!"

Crashing waves add beats to the tune,
As night crabs dance under the silver moon.
Perhaps a mermaid will drop by to tease,
With a whirl and a twirl that aims to please.

Carols of the Waving Palms

In the breeze, the palms hum a song,
While lizards strut, thinking they're strong.
Coconuts plop as they laugh and roll,
In a tropical dance that never gets old.

Sandy toes tap to the rhythm they hear,
As parrots squawk, spreading good cheer.
The sun smiles bright, a jester in disguise,
In a canopy of colors that almost flies.

Breeze whispers jokes through the tangled leaves,
As beachgoers giggle, rolling up their sleeves.
The scent of salt mixes with glee,
In this playful world, forever carefree.

A hammock sways like a friendly wave,
As crickets compete with the songs they gave.
Underneath skies so wide and bold,
The palms keep secrets, forever untold.

Fleeting Melodies of Misty Horizons

Clouds drift lazily, forming a band,
While sea sprites frolic, hand in hand.
A lighthouse beams with a wink and a nod,
As waves sway softly, giving a applaud.

Tiny boats bob like corks in tea,
While gulls join the chorus, setting hearts free.
Each splash is a laugh that tickles the air,
As sunsets paint stories with colors so rare.

Beneath the mist, whispers play,
With sea turtles sneaking a late-night stay.
The horizon hums a jazzy delight,
As bubbles burst from laughter so bright.

These fleeting moments can't be contained,
As crabs hold contests for the sand they've gained.
In this realm of giggles and dreams,
Life's a melody bursting at the seams.

Oceanic Verses

In a boat made of cheese,
With a captain who sneezes,
We sail through the jelly,
And dance with the medley.

Seagulls dive for our fries,
With their highly trained eyes,
They squawk and they dive-bomb,
While we try to stay calm.

The waves tickle our toes,
As we giggle in prose,
Our sunscreen is melted,
And our plans are shelved.

When the fish start to chatter,
And the dolphins know better,
We join their parade,
Under sun's playful shade.

Saltwater Serenities

From a beach chair so wide,
I watch kids take a ride,
On a crab with a hat,
Who insists he's not fat.

The ocean waves clap cheer,
As the sandcastles leer,
A sandman starts to dance,
And we all join the prance.

Lost sunglasses parade,
In the tide's grand charade,
Waves crash with a giggle,
And we all start to wiggle.

Turtle races ensue,
With a snail's point of view,
We place our bets anew,
On who'll pass the blue goo.

Windswept Chants

Oh the breeze so surreal,
Brought us chips for a meal,
The seagulls start a band,
With their potato stand.

My hat flies far away,
It's joined a crab ballet,
I chase it through the brine,
While laughing at its line.

Fish sing songs of delight,
To the moon's gentle light,
Finding rhythm in waves,
And joy in the caves.

When the tide starts to groove,
And all creatures approve,
We laugh with the sea,
In our whimsical spree.

The Chorus of the Coral

Underwater, they grin,
The clams squawk a din,
As fish form a choir,
Their scales catching fire.

A starfish spins a tale,
Of a snail on a rail,
Who rode through the blue,
With a shoe made for two.

The octopus plays drums,
As the clownfish hums,
Their laughter resounds,
In the underwater towns.

Every seaweed sways,
To the rhythm of days,
In this raucous ballet,
Where humor holds sway.

Close to the Current

On a boat shaped like a shoe,
We paddle past a floating zoo.
Fish wave at us with silly grins,
While mermaids laugh at our clumsy spins.

Sailing close to the raucous shore,
A seagull steals our lunch once more.
We chase it down, what a sight!
Sandwiches flying, oh what a flight!

The sun is bright, the sky is blue,
Our captain looks like a kangaroo.
With every splash, our worries drift,
In this silly boat, we get a lift.

As we sail and start to cheer,
A dolphin jumps, not far from here.
He shows us tricks with a joyful spin,
In this watery playground, let the fun begin!

Melodies of the Misty Isles

In the mist of the morning light,
A crab sings songs that feel just right.
He taps his claws with a rhythmic beat,
While jellyfish dance with flappy feet.

The trees sway like they're in a trance,
As turtles join in the merry dance.
They shake their shells and click their heels,
In this party, everything appeals!

A parrot struts, all feathers bright,
Telling jokes that are quite a sight.
He squawks, "Why don't fish play guitar?
Because they're afraid of the bass guitar!"

The waves clap hands, the sun shines wide,
Laughter echoes with the ocean's tide.
In this misty world of quirky glee,
Every note feels so carefree!

The Reverie of Rising Tides

With every wave, a giggling sound,
The beach ball dances round and round.
A crab in shades takes a sunlit stroll,
Pretending to be the life of the shoal.

As tides rise high, we start a race,
Splashing water all over the place.
Our fins are flailing, so full of cheer,
Even the fish start to cheer us near.

The sun dips low, its colors bloom,
While starfish twirl in the evening's gloom.
Each creature here just wants to play,
Merriment blooms like the end of the day.

A whale tells tales of ocean gold,
Of pirate treasure and secrets old.
We roll in the sand, laughter untied,
In the carefree moment of rising tide!

Harmony of the Horizon

At the edge where the sea meets the sky,
A pelican fluffs, oh how it does fly!
With a flip of a wing, it starts to dive,
In this land of laughter, we feel alive.

The tide pulls back with a playful sweep,
A sandcastle stands, but it can't keep.
The clumsy crabs give it a shake,
Until it tumbles like a giant cake.

Under palm trees, we tell tall tales,
Of fish that ride on the backs of snails.
The breeze carries giggles, it sways our toes,
In this silly realm where laughter grows.

As colors dance on the horizon bright,
Seagulls sing songs of pure delight.
Each moment passes like a whimsical rhyme,
In this fun-filled place, we bide our time!

Secrets of the Surf

Waves whisper tales, they giggle and sway,
A crab in a tux, he's ready to play.
Seagulls are gossiping, flying about,
While sunbathers wonder what's that loud shout.

Fish in the sea, they dance and they spin,
Teaching dolphins how to wear a grin.
The surfboard broke, but hey, what a ride!
Splashing your buddy, with cheer, not with pride.

Shells hide secrets with plenty of sass,
A clam tells jokes, with a smile so brash.
While starfish are lounging, deeply they dream,
In a world full of laughter, nothing's as it seems.

So grab a cold drink, let your troubles slide,
Join the ocean's concert, it's one fun ride!
From barnacle bands to the foghorn's low tune,
The secrets of surf are a fantastic cartoon!

Breezy Ballads of Belief

The wind whispers sweet, with tales of the jest,
A kite caught my heart, it just wouldn't rest.
Sandy toes tap to tunes of delight,
While turtles attempt to join in the flight.

Palm trees sway gently, they're dancing in line,
As donkeys on surfboards are stealing the shine.
The breeze plays the lute, mellows out every frown,
And piña coladas make worries wash down.

Laughter erupts as a seagull takes food,
He's the pirate tonight, oh, such a rude dude!
Beachball ballet, oh, what a show,
With sandcastles wobbling, they steal the glow.

So join in the breezy, jubilant spree,
Where laughter and joy hold the master key.
Together we sing, in the sunlight's warm light,
Breezy ballads of belief that feel just right!

The Ebb and Flow of Feelings

Tides pull my heart, like an old worn-out sock,
Sometimes it's a giggle, sometimes, a mock.
A wave rolls in, says, "Don't be a fool!"
While jellyfish giggle, stating, "We rule!"

The seafoam whispers, "What's drowning your cheer?"
As crabs throw a party, they invite you near.
Surfboards collide, much to everyone's shock,
And laughter erupts like a clock with no tick-tock.

Seagulls are jesters, with jokes to lay bare,
While sand buckets chuckle with every last glare.
The ebb and the flow, it's a comedy scene,
Where feelings are tossed like a frisbee of green.

So ride all the currents, jump high with a shout,
The ocean's a stage, come and flip your doubt!
With every laugh breaking like waves on the sand,
The ebb and the flow—we'll forever withstand!

Driftwood Dreams

Driftwood rolls in with a wise, goofy grin,
Claiming he's king, what a swell way to win!
Barnacles gather, they form a new crew,
With oceanic humor and shells shiny blue.

Sandcastles rise, then laugh when they fall,
The tide sneaks up, plays the sneakiest call.
Pineapple hats on the old driftwood king,
While starfish applaud, it's a comical thing!

Hovering seagulls add flair to the show,
As starry-eyed dreamers go with the flow.
Shells whisper secrets, drifting off in a sweep,
Driftwood dreams churn in their oceanic sleep.

So let the waves cradle your fanciful thoughts,
In a land where laughter ties all of the knots.
From sand to the sea, let the joy take a stand,
Where driftwood gathers with wonders so grand!

Choral Waves Crashing Onshore

The waves sing loud, they splash and roar,
An otter dances on the sandy floor.
With seagulls laughing in the sun's warm glow,
They twirl and leap, putting on a show.

A crab in a tux, he moves with style,
While seashells giggle, going the extra mile.
Jellyfish jam to the bubbles' beat,
Their gooey moves are truly hard to greet.

A sailor slips with grand aplomb,
As fish toss confetti, a slippery bomb.
The ocean hums a tune so bright,
As clams compose, from morning till night.

With tunes so sweet, the shore's alive,
Every creature has joined in the jive.
The tide rolls in with a slippery cheer,
Embracing the humor, year after year.

Symphonies of the Swaying Grasses

The grasses sway, a gentle ballet,
They dip and dive in a breezy play.
A squirrel conducts with an acorn baton,
While ants march in line, a tiny polygon.

The flowers giggle, dressed in bright hues,
With bees in top hats, singing the blues.
The breeze whistles tunes, it's quite a delight,
As dandelions puff, taking flight.

A chicken clucks, with rhythm so bold,
Sharing her wisdom, stories untold.
While frogs play drums on a lily-pad stage,
Their croaks and splashes are all the rage.

Each rustling leaf joins the quirky refrain,
In this grassy land, it's all fun and gain.
With nature's orchestra making a scene,
The concert continues, pure and serene.

Rhymes of the Crystal Lagoons

In a lagoon bright, where laughter grows,
The ducks wear shades, striking silly poses.
Mermaids giggle at splashing fish,
As bubbles rise up, granting each wish.

A turtle spins tales, oh what a sight,
While flamingos stretch, all decked in pink light.
Coconuts find their groove with a twist,
Dancing all day, they simply can't resist.

The water shimmers, reflecting the fun,
Where everything sparkles beneath the sun.
But watch out for crabs, in a misfit crew,
With dance moves so wild, they just might ensue.

Laughter and splashes fill the lagoon air,
Everyone's invited, let down your hair.
With funny antics, the day's never lost,
In this wacky paradise, we'll never exhaust.

Odes from the Drifting Clouds

Up in the sky, where the clouds drift by,
A ballet of dreams, off the feathered high.
Cotton candy puffs enjoying a ride,
While sunbeams gossip, taking joy in their stride.

A balloon floats past, with a goofy grin,
Chasing the laughter among the chagrin.
Raindrops twirl like dancers in flight,
Creating a rhythm as day turns to night.

Thunder clouds giggle, a rumbling tune,
As lightning plays games, lighting up the moon.
The wind whirls around, with a cheeky embrace,
While clouds share secrets in their fluffy space.

With hearts full of mirth, they float to the ends,
Each puffy formation just drifts and bends.
In this sky of comedy, life takes its aim,
As the clouds sing loud, never feeling lame.

Cadence of the Salty Air

The seagulls squawk with flair,
Their feathers tossed in the breeze,
Crabs dance a jig with no care,
While the waves play tag with the trees.

Sunburned tourists in a race,
Chasing shadows, losing hats,
With ice cream drips on their face,
And laughter shared among the brats.

A dolphin flips with a grin,
Splashing water on a sunbather,
While the fish roll round in sin,
Wondering who's their next slather.

Shells whisper secrets so bright,
Telling tales of days gone past,
While the tide hums late at night,
Hoping this moment will last.

Rhythmic Secrets of Hidden Arches

Beneath the rocks, a crab's scuttle,
Sketches rhythms in the sand,
A starfish joins in the huddle,
As they form a band so grand.

Sunsets drip like melting cheese,
Sizzling skies in shades of fun,
Waves that dance with goofy ease,
While the gulls just laugh and run.

A treasure map with a twist,
Points to where the snacks are hid,
Pirates laugh and shake their fists,
As the jellybeans are bid.

Turtles glide with gentle grace,
In a swim that looks like a waltz,
While the sea cows join the race,
Leaving bubbles, not their faults.

Dances of the Whispering Winds

The palm trees twist in cheeky style,
As the breeze wraps 'round like a hug,
Clouds gather like a curious file,
And the sun is a grinning slug.

Shells spin tales at watery bars,
As fish wear hats made of foam,
Starlit nights shine like bizarre,
As whispers in the night roam.

Laughter bubbles up from below,
Where the octopus shows off flair,
With each twist and every flow,
Echoing joy in the salty air.

The wind takes every song it knows,
Mixing humor in each warm gust,
Heartfelt whistles, soft to those,
Chasing giggles, fun is a must.

Echoing Shores of Lost Dreams

Footprints washed by the tide,
Where kids build castles, then flee,
Laughter echoing far and wide,
As kites dance wild, oh so free.

Seashells giggle in the light,
Holding secrets, stories grand,
Hiding inside with delight,
A world crafted from the sand.

The sunset's a clown in the sky,
Painting giggles across the blue,
While mermaids wink as they fly,
Waving to those who dream true.

Footloose and fancy, the waves tease,
Tickling toes on the shore's gleam,
In this land of smiles and ease,
The echoes hold warmth like a dream.

The Melody of Mistral

A breeze comes dancing on the bay,
Whispers secrets in a playful way.
The gulls are laughing, a funny sight,
Chasing each other, pure delight.

The palm trees sway, a comical show,
As if they're grooving, don't you know?
The waves join in, they clap and cheer,
While crabs groove sideways, never fear!

Fish in the sea are quite the jest,
Popping up just to take a rest.
They wiggle and squirm with silly grace,
In this sea of laughter, we embrace.

So let's rise up with a bubbly cheer,
With every wave that draws us near.
In the melody where humor sings,
Life's a dance with delightful flings.

Quietude Amongst the Mangroves

In shadows deep where laughter hides,
The mangroves whisper, and mischief abides.
A monkey swings with acrobatic flair,
Telling tales to the crabs unaware.

Frogs croak in sync, an odd little band,
Each note a hiccup, quite unplanned.
The turtles chuckle, slow and proud,
While the mudskippers jive, they're not too loud.

The gnarled roots twist like a jester's hat,
As kingfishers dive with a splish and a splat.
Nature's comedy plays without delay,
In this quiet nook where fun finds a way.

So bask in the giggles, the humor profound,
As each creature shares laughter all around.
Amidst the green, our spirits rise,
In this serene jest, our joy complies.

Nautical Nocturne

Under the stars, the ships do sway,
Mermaids giddy with tales of the day.
Their laughter echoes through the moonlight,
Splashing and giggling, what a sight!

The fishermen snore with their nets all round,
While seagulls plot mischief, making sound.
A fish pops up, wearing a grin,
"Catch me if you can!" is the game they spin.

The waves tickle toes and dance with delight,
Creating shadows that jump in the night.
The anchor's off, but spirits are high,
As laughter collides with a winking sky.

So let the night be a playful stage,
Where every creature beams with glee, not rage.
In this nautical dance, let's make a toast,
To the funny moments we treasure most!

A Tune from the Tidepools

In tidepools bright, the crabs have a ball,
Tap dancing joyfully, oh, what a call!
Starfish twirl in their mottled attire,
While anemones giggle, they never tire.

The seashells clatter in rhythmic delight,
Joining the chorus, what a funny sight!
Waves take a bow, then crash in jest,
As oceanic friends have a fun little fest.

A fishy trio harmonizes with flair,
While seagulls squawk in the salty air.
It's a cacophony of glee, no less,
In nature's concert, we feel truly blessed.

So dip your toes in the merriment near,
Catch the tide's humor, let out a cheer.
For in these pools of laughter and light,
Fun blooms and bubbles all through the night.

Whispering Tides

The waves giggle with glee,
As crabs dance on the sand.
Seagulls squawk a silly tune,
While fish flip in the breeze.

Shells wear hats of bright colors,
Jellyfish float like balloons.
Starfish play peek-a-boo,
Under the sun's warm glows.

Turtles race in slow motion,
While the tide tickles toes.
The beach ball's a rolling star,
In this fun-filled sandy show.

Coconuts chuckle loudly,
As coconut milk splashes wide.
Each wave brings a new riddle,
Where laughter can't safely hide.

Echoes of the Ebb

The breeze tells jokes to the palm trees,
While crickets join in the fun.
There's a crab with a tiny crown,
Claiming he's king of the run.

Splashing waves make funny faces,
As if splashed with a grin.
A sea turtle sings softly,
Till the seagulls join in the din.

Footprints lead to nowhere,
As if lost in a chase.
A sandcastle winks at the tide,
Proud of its sandy face.

A clumsy pelican dives too low,
Then flaps to find his way.
Echoes of laughter resound,
In this oceanic play.

Evening Chants at Dusk

As the sun sinks low and smiles,
The waves hum a silly verse.
Fireflies join in the dance,
While the moon practices a rehearse.

Pineapples wear little hats,
While mangoes take a stroll.
Coconuts gossip in whispers,
Under the nighttime scroll.

A chorus of croaking frogs,
Sings tunes of the salty day.
Crabs shuffle their tiny feet,
As if they've lost their way.

The stars wink down in laughter,
As night blankets the shore.
Evening chants bring out the fun,
Like never seen before.

Shoreside Symphony

The beach band strums a tune,
With shells as their finest flutes.
Drums made of seawater buckets,
Make music without disputes.

A dandy crab takes the lead,
With moves that steal the show.
While tiny fish swim along,
In a synchronized flow.

Starfish clap their little hands,
Joining in the lively beat.
Sandcastles nod their own heads,
To the rhythm of beachy heat.

The sunset paints with gold,
As laughter fills the air.
A shoreside symphony plays,
With joy beyond compare.

The Murmur of Moonlit Waters

The fish wear tuxedos, all ready to dance,
As crabs do the cha-cha in a curious prance.
The moon's a DJ, spinning tunes through the night,
While dolphins throw parties with bubbles and light.

The seaweed's a curtain, the waves take a bow,
The seagulls are judges with notepads somehow.
They hoot and they holler, all critiquing with glee,
To be part of this circus, oh how fun to be free!

Starfish are bouncers, they stand by the door,
With starry-eyed fish getting ready for more.
The shells sing a chorus, the tide keeps the beat,
So come join the fun, end your day on this street!

As laughter erupts from the salty old sea,
Under moonlit reflections, life's fanciful spree.
So float on your raft of carefree delight,
With giggles and splashes, we vanish from sight.

Waves of Whispered Secrets

The sand's got a secret, it tickles your toes,
While crabs shout their gossip in high-pitched meows.
The tide brings a tale, all frothy and bright,
Of mermaids who frolic under the starlight.

The conch shell's a phone, it rings with a shout,
"Hey barnacles, guess what? Can you come out?"
The sea cucumbers roll with laughter and cheer,
As jellyfish giggle, they wiggle with flair.

The pelicans dive, with a splash and a wink,
Their jokes are fishy, but we're still in sync.
Octopus waiter serves squid with a grin,
"Best catch of the day! Come join us, jump in!"

With waves whispering secrets, we float on the breeze,
In a world full of fun, we dance with such ease.
Under the soft glow of the warm summer light,
Come share in the joy, let's party all night!

Maritime Musings

A parrot recites from a worn-out old book,
Of pirates who never knew how to cook.
They'd feast on the seaweed, with laughter and glee,
And barter for treasure with cups of sweet tea.

The seahorses gallop, like horses on land,
With a sense of pure wonder, they trot through the sand.
They gather in circles, discussing the tide,
And gossip about fish who always tried to hide.

The tides bring in stories, like letters from friends,
Of starry-eyed dolphins who're hoping for bends.
They leap through the flavors of salt and of cheer,
In laughter and splashes, they sense that we're near.

So let's raise a toast to the waves and the sea,
To tales carved in foam, as silly as can be.
With each frothy whisper, our hearts start to soar,
In maritime musings, there's always much more!

Sun-Kissed Soliloquies

Beneath the bright sun, the clams form a band,
With rhythm and shells, they create quite a strand.
They jam with the crabs, in a sandy café,
With melodies drifting, we dance 'til the day.

The umbrellas all giggle, caught in a breeze,
As seagulls drive cabs and fly with such ease.
With surfboards for sails, they glide with delight,
In the fun of the moment, everything feels right.

The coconuts chatter, debating the weather,
While sunbeams are casting warm rays altogether.
The tide hums a tune, a serenade sweet,
As shells hold the stories of laughter and heat.

So here's to the moments, sun-kissed on the shore,
With goofy smiles shining, who could ask for more?
Join in the soliloquies, carefree and bright,
Together in laughter, we dance through the night!

Shores of Solitude

A crab on the beach is dancing slow,
With clumsy moves, it steals the show.
Waves applaud with a gentle hush,
While seagulls mimic in a silly rush.

The sunburnt tourists wear socks with sandals,
Searching for ice cream, leaving scandals.
A flip flop flies, a moment of flight,
Lands on the dog, oh what a sight!

Sandcastles rise with moats of pride,
Till the tide comes in, like a cheeky ride.
Children squeal as they splash and play,
Underneath the sun's bright ray.

As the evening falls, we gather 'round,
Telling stories of the funny sounds.
Waves chuckle softly, the stars are bright,
On these shores, everything feels right.

The Lullaby of Distant Waves

A turtle snores in a sunbeam's glow,
Dreaming of places where sea cucumbers grow.
The fish cheer loud with bubbles and glee,
While octopus laughs, 'Come dance with me!'

A parrot mimics a phone that rings,
For cocktail orders, it hilariously sings.
With every squawk, it's a jolly spree,
As pirates roll by in a made-up decree.

Napping on hammocks, no cares in sight,
Bananarama plays, turning wrongs to right.
In the distance, a yacht sails on by,
With a cat on deck, plotting mischief sly.

As night draws close, the moon starts to play,
Reflecting wishes on the waters' sway.
With laughter and joy, we'll all embrace,
This silly rhythm, a warm, happy place.

Echoes in the Breeze

Whispers of wind share secrets so sly,
As kites dance wildly, soaring high.
An ice cream cone melts at an alarming rate,
As seagulls dive down, plotting fate.

The sun hats spin, a wacky parade,
While flip-flops squeak, with trades made.
Sandy toes peek from beneath the chair,
While folks swap tales without a care.

Drifting coconut floats on by,
With a smiley face, oh my oh my!
The rhythm of laughter fills the warm air,
As crabs paint their shells with playful flair.

As day slips away, the lanterns glow,
Flickering bright in a jovial show.
With echoes of joy riding the breeze,
We toast to the silly moments like these.

An Overture Beneath the Palms

A monkey swings with an acorn hat,
Chasing after bright shiny that.
Palm leaves rustle a tune so sweet,
As lizards dance to the syncopate beat.

Picnic blankets are fidgeting about,
Searching for snacks that were truly devout.
A sandwich escapes, it rolls away fast,
Chasing down shadows, a laugh unsurpassed.

The sun dips low, painting skies with grace,
As jellyfish waltz in an ocean embrace.
Bubbles erupt from beneath the foam,
Turning the sea into a hiccupping home.

As night unfolds with stars that wink,
Seashells gather for a nightly drink.
Under the palms, we giggle and sway,
In this overture, we'll surely stay.

www.ingramcontent.com/pod-product-compliance
Lightning Source LLC
Chambersburg PA
CBHW072119070526
44585CB00016B/1503